KEYBOARD *signature licks*

BEST ROCK

by Todd Lowry

ISBN 0-634-05636-0

HAL•LEONARD®
CORPORATION
7777 W. BLUEMOUND RD. P.O. BOX 13819 MILWAUKEE, WI 53213

Visit Hal Leonard Online at
www.halleonard.com

TABLE OF CONTENTS

INTRODUCTION

This book/CD is a guide to various keyboard styles and techniques used by several of the giants of rock music. The artists included in this book encompass nearly three decades of music and a wide variety of styles. We've chosen songs that are particularly keyboard-oriented. The keyboards used include acoustic piano, electric piano, synthesizer, organ, and accordion.

A study of the keyboard styles herein reveals a rich harmonic vocabulary, frequently incorporating inversions, extended chords, slash chords, add9 chords, pedal tones, and unique chord progressions.

That said, the songs in this book are basically *pop* songs, and the keyboard parts serve the overall effect of the songs. Therefore, most of the examples in this book consist of *comping* patterns. "Comping" is musicians' lingo for "accompaniment," and a comping pattern is a rhythmic and harmonic background for the vocal melody. A wide variety of comping styles are found here, including block chords, repeated chords, broken chords, left-hand octave patterns, boogie-woogie patterns, blues licks, and parallel 3rds in the right hand. Many of these songs also have introductions and/or instrumental interludes that showcase the keyboards.

The music herein is certain to be around for generations. Hopefully, this book will contribute to the appreciation and understanding of it.

THE RECORDING

Follow the audio track icons ◆ in the book to find your spot on the CD. The icons are placed after the figure numbers at the top of each figure. When more than one icon appears after a figure, the first track listed is a recording of the figure in full, and the following tracks are notable individual keyboard parts played as slow demos. Featured keyboard parts on the full-band tracks are isolated on one side of the stereo mix, so you can isolate them for closer study, or pan them out and jam along with the band when you have learned the parts.

Warren Wiegratz–Keyboards
Doug Boduch–Guitars
Tom McGirr–Bass
Scott Schroedl–Drums
Recorded, mixed, and mastered by Jim Reith at Beathouse Music, Milwaukee, WI

BLOODY WELL RIGHT
From the Supertramp album *Crime of the Century* (1974)
Words and Music by Rick Davies and Roger Hodgson

Formed in London in 1969, Supertramp took its name from the 1910 W.H. Davies book *The Autobiography of a Supertramp*. The keyboard-dominated "Bloody Well Right" was a top 40 hit in 1975.

Figure 1–Intro and Guitar Solo

Notice the *swing eighths* marking after the tempo indication; this means that whenever you see eighth notes, they are to be played as swing eighths. That is, the second of each pair of eighth notes is played on the last *third* of a triplet, rather than in the middle of the beat. In jazz, swing, and rock shuffles, there is always an underlying triplet feel.

The intro begins with a long Wurlitzer electric piano solo based on the alternation of two chords, Fm7 and B♭, and is punctuated by occasional loud punches by the band. The key signature is three flats, but the song is actually in the B♭ Mixolydian mode (i.e., the B♭ major scale with an A♭ instead of A♮).

The piano solo is a compilation of blues-like piano techniques. First, there is the use of *grace notes* in measures 1 and 7, especially leading from the ♭3rd (C♯) to the ♮3rd (D) of the key. Grace notes are quick ornamental tones played directly before a main note. The two (or more) notes are usually connected with a small slur marking. Grace notes are sometimes called "crushed notes," and we also refer to the use of a grace note as "bending a note," because it sounds similar to a guitar player bending a note.

Second, there is heavy use of the G blues scale. (G is the relative minor of B♭ major.) Both the lick in measure 2 and the passage in measures 8–12 are based on the G blues scale.

Third, is the use of double notes with blues licks in measures 10, 13–14, and 16–19. The blues lick appears in the lower part, while the 5th of the key (F) is repeated on top. The quarter-note triplet rhythm beginning at measure 26 is also a standard blues technique, as are the blues scale licks in octaves at measures 33–34, the bluesy turns at measures 4 and 13, and the use of 3rds in measures 18 and 29.

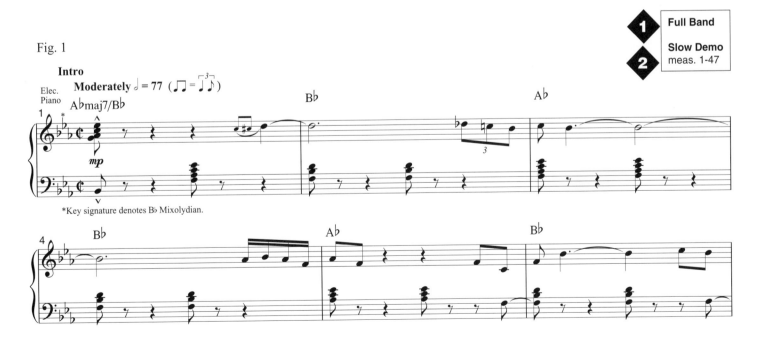

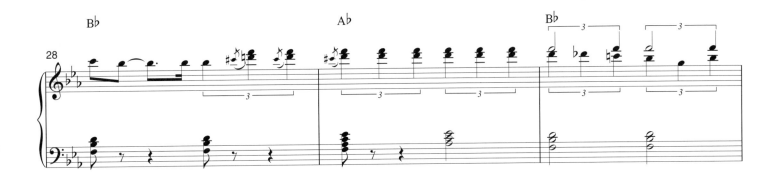

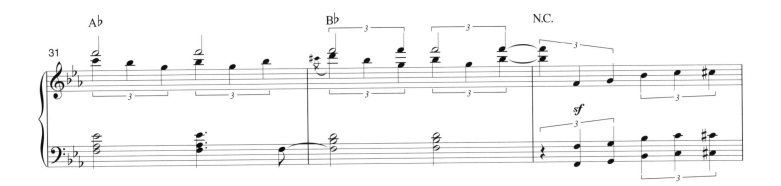

Guitar Solo 0:54

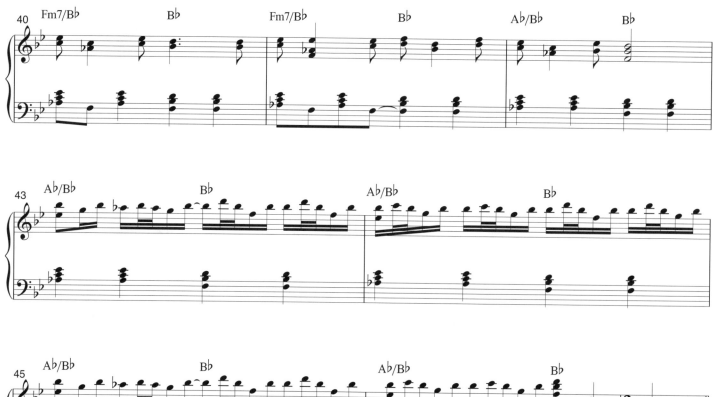

Figure 2–Chorus

After the hard-rocking verse, the chorus feels rather jaunty. In the first four measures, triads are played by the right hand in an eighth-note rhythm in the upper register of the piano, with the left hand basically doubling the pattern on electric piano one octave lower. In the successive measures, the left hand plays the triads, with broken chord fills in the right hand.

3 Full Band

4 Slow Demo
Piano   meas. 5-9

Fig. 2

Right,_____ you're blood-y well right, you know you got a right to say._____

Right, _ you're blood-y well right, you know you got a right _ to say. _

Ha, ha, you're blood-y well right, you know you're right to say. _

Yeh, yeh, you're blood-y well ___ right, ___

you know you're right to say. _ And me I don't care an-y-way.

COLD AS ICE
From the Foreigner album *Foreigner* (1977)
Words and Music by Mick Jones and Lou Gramm

Formed in New York in 1976, Foreigner derived its name from the fact that the original members were from both sides of the Atlantic. With their memorable melodic hooks and intelligently crafted sound, Foreigner epitomizes the classic sound of AOR (Album-Oriented Rock), and was a prime staple of 1970s and 1980s American FM radio. "Cold as Ice" was a hit single in 1977.

Figure 3–Intro, Verse 1, Verse 2, Guitar Solo, and Chorus

The intro begins with insistent chords alternating between E♭sus4 and E♭m in the right hand of the piano, with octaves in the left hand. This pattern continues in the verse with the additional harmonies of C♭6 and C♭. At measure 12, the organ enters with triad punches on beats 2 and 4. In the second part of the verse (beginning at meas. 18), triads in the piano and organ are held for four beats. At measure 26, the intro figure appears again with the addition of a synthesizer in the baritone range playing a melodic fill.

Verse two (meas. 30) isn't much different from verse one, except for the addition of the synthesizer playing a fill at measure 35. The piano continues its quarter-note chords even during the guitar solo at measure 51.

The chorus switches to a half-time feel and makes use of *slash chords.* A slash chord is a chord with a note other than the root in the bass. Slash chords spice up a chord progression and can make the bass line more interesting. Here, slash chords such as B♭/F and B♭7/A♭ are used to good effect.

Fig. 3

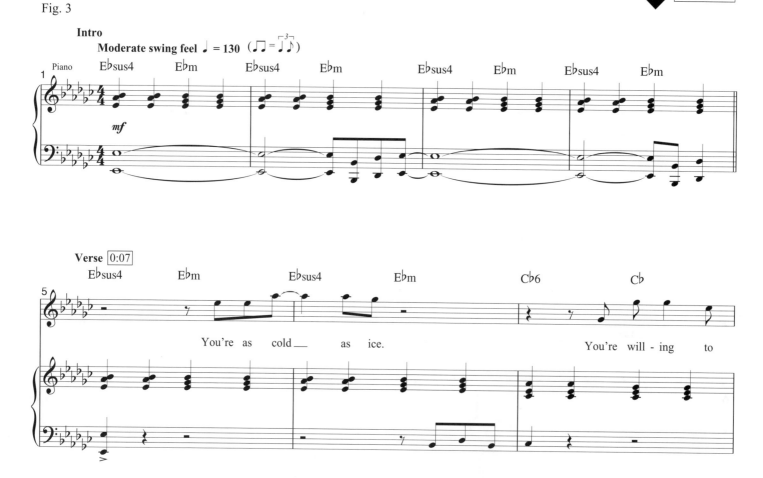

sac - ri - fice __ our love. __

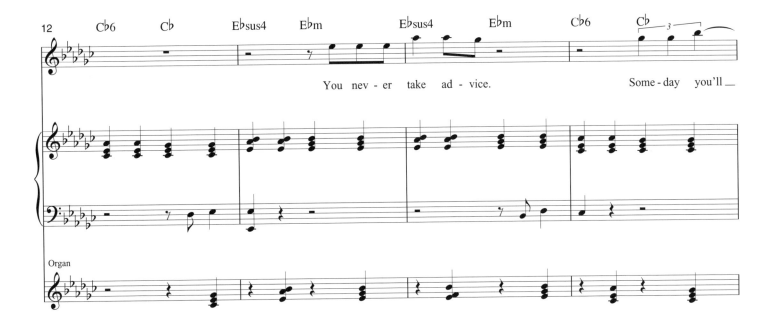

You nev - er take ad - vice. Some - day you'll __

__ pay the price, __ I know. I've seen it be - fore, __ it hap - pens all the time. You're

closing the door,— you leave the world be-hind.— You're dig-ging for gold,— yet

throw-ing a-way— a for-tune in feel - ings, but some-day you'll pay.

Organ tacet

Synth.

Verse 0:53

You're as cold___ as ice. You're will-ing to sac-ri-fice___ our love.___

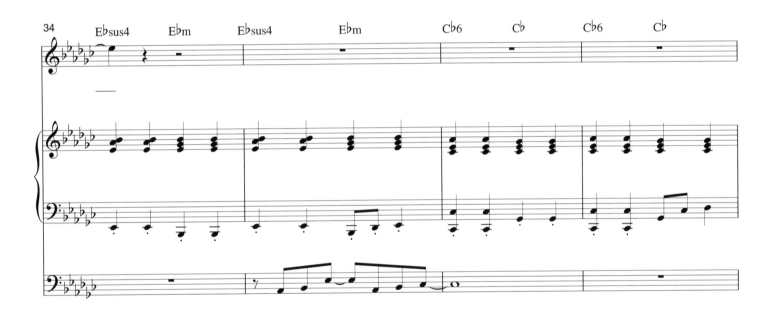

You want par-a-dise, but some-day you'll___ pay the price___ I

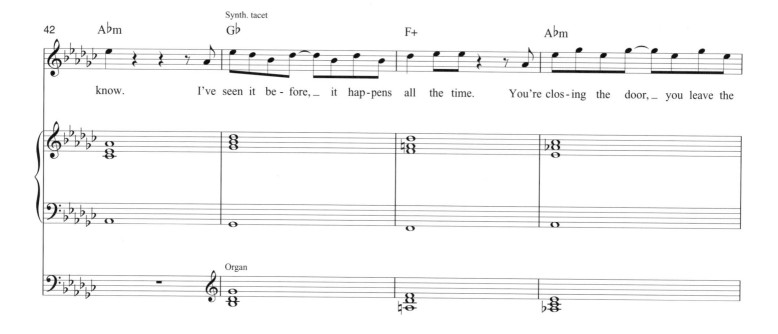

know. I've seen it be-fore,_ it hap-pens all the time. You're clos-ing the door,_ you leave the

world be-hind.___ You're dig-ging for gold,_ yet throw-ing a-way___ a

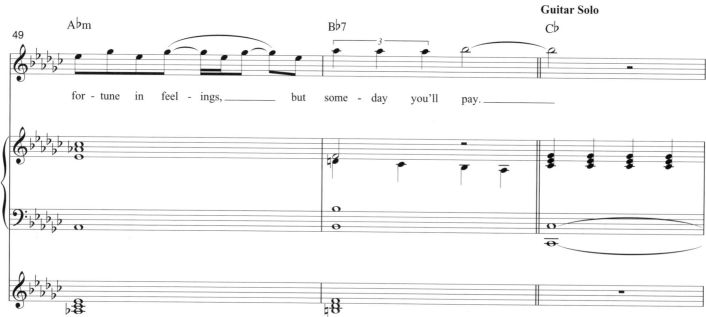

for-tune in feel-ings,_____ but some-day you'll pay._____

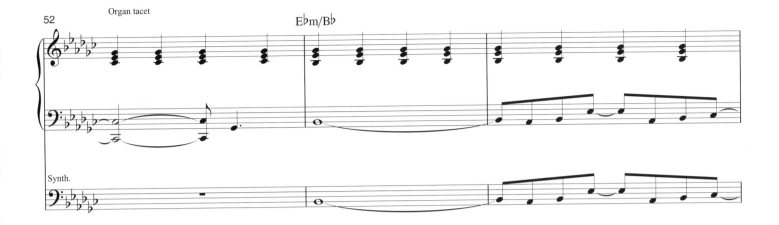

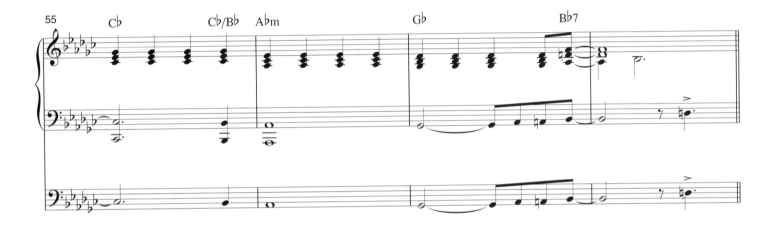

Chorus 1:47

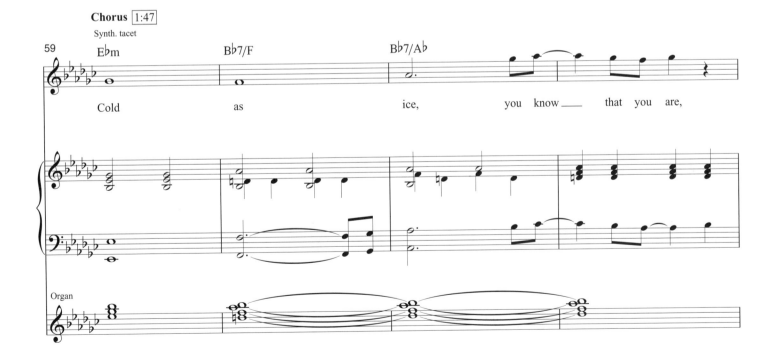

Cold as ice, you know ___ that you are,

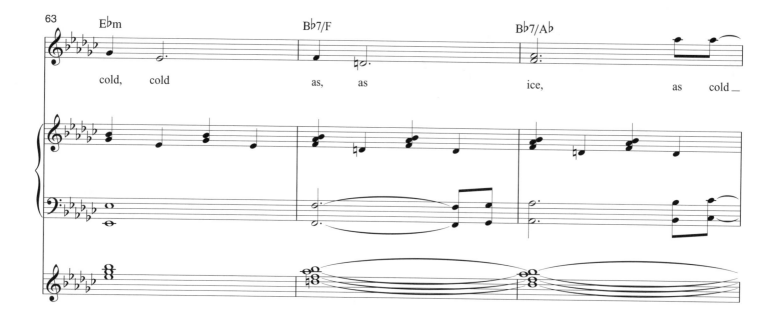

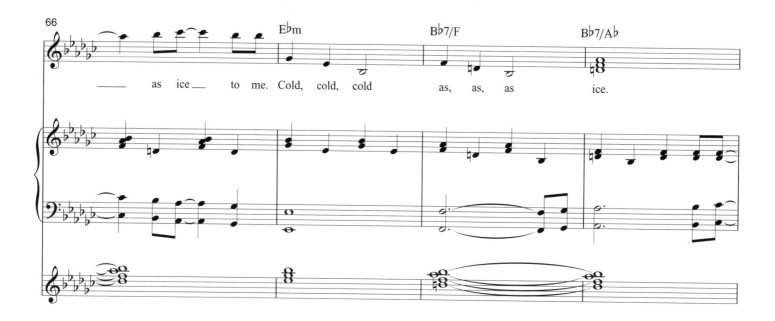

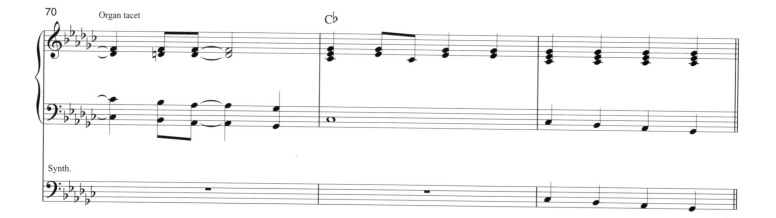

DON'T DO ME LIKE THAT
From the Tom Petty & The Heartbreakers album
Damn the Torpedoes (1979)
Words and Music by Tom Petty

Tom Petty formed the Heartbreakers in 1976. Armed with a Rickenbacker guitar and a voice reminiscent of Roger McGuinn, Petty and company were often compared to the Byrds. With his irresistible hook lines and unpretentious rock, Petty appealed to both new-wavers and lovers of roots-oriented rock 'n' roll.

Figure 4–Intro, Verse, and Chorus

The song begins with a four-chord pattern (G–Fmaj7–Am/C–Am/D) that will be the basis for the verse. The right hand plays triads repeated in an eighth-note rhythm in the soprano register of the piano, with a syncopated bass line in the left hand. Organ is added on the repeat of the first four measures of the intro. Measure 1 (on the repeat) features an organ "fall-off" or downward *glissando* (abbreviated as *gliss.* and represented in notation by the wavy line). The glissando is a classic blues and rock keyboard device: a rapid scale passage accomplished by quickly sliding the hands over the keys (usually on the white keys, although black-key glissandos are also possible). For this "fall-off," or descending gliss., use the nail of the right thumb to quickly descend the keys.

The chorus changes only slightly from the verse with the insertion of an Em chord in the progression. The organ simply holds triads. The piano fills in measures 16 and 20 are based on the G major pentatonic scale (G–A–B–D–E).

6	**Full Band**
7	**Slow Demo** Piano meas. 13-20

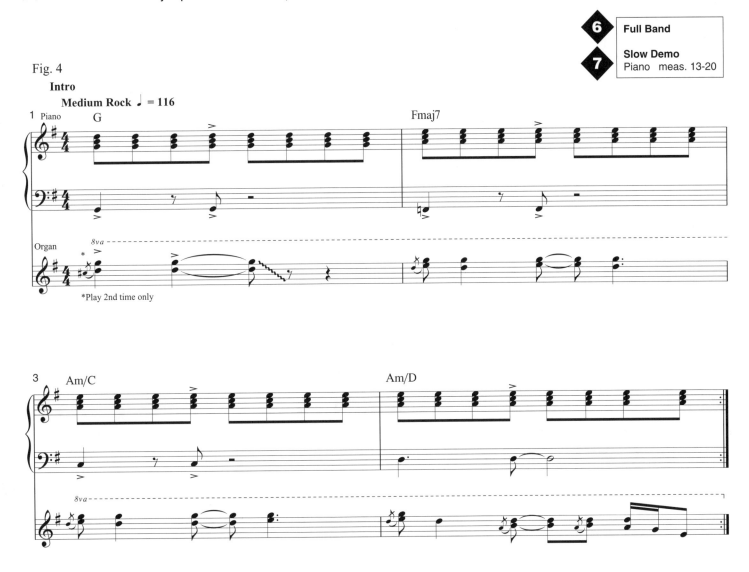

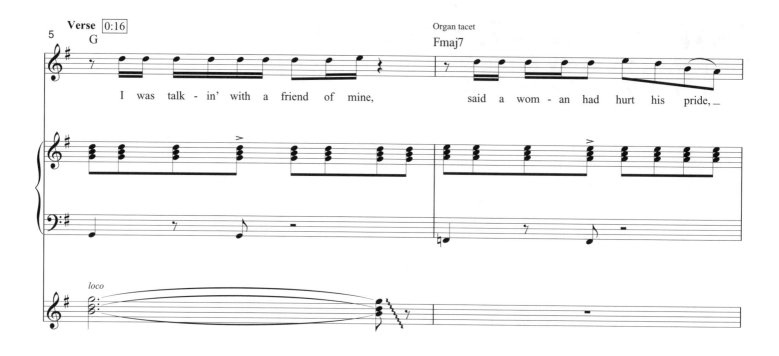

Verse 0:16

Organ tacet

I was talk - in' with a friend of mine, said a wom - an had hurt his pride, __

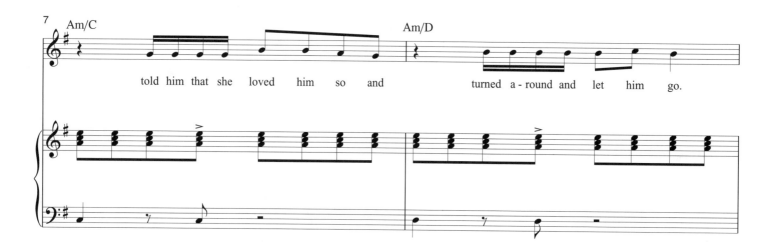

told him that she loved him so and turned a - round and let him go.

Then he said, "You bet - ter watch your step, or you're gon - na get hurt your - self. __

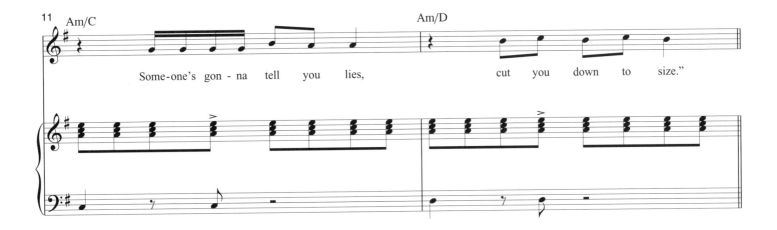

Some-one's gon - na tell you lies,   cut you down to size."

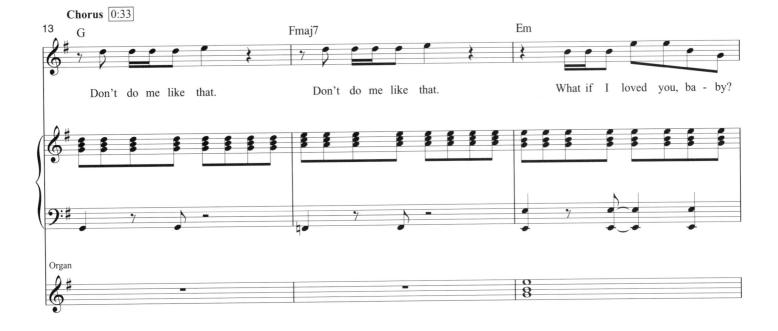

Chorus `0:33`

Don't do me like that.   Don't do me like that.   What if I loved you, ba - by?

Organ

Don't do me like that.   Don't do me like that.   Don't do me like that.

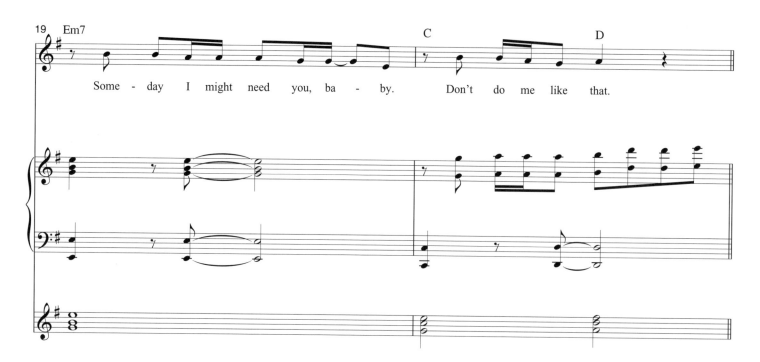

Some - day I might need you, ba - by. Don't do me like that.

Figure 5–Bridge

The bridge features blues-like elements including both I7 and IV7 chords, the "blues note" alternation between B in the G7 chord and B♭ in the C7 chord, and "bends" from A♯ into B on the G7 chords.

The "garage band" organ riff in measures 2, 4, and 6 works well in this context.

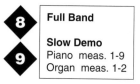

8 Full Band

9 Slow Demo
Piano meas. 1-9
Organ meas. 1-2

Fig. 5

Bridge 1:22

'Cause some - where deep, down ___ in - side, ___ some - one is say - in', "Love ___

DON'T LET THE SUN GO DOWN ON ME

From the Elton John album *Caribou* (1974)
Words and Music by Elton John and Bernie Taupin

"Don't Let the Sun Go Down on Me" is a sweeping, panoramic ballad. It covers a wide range of emotions, from hurt in the first verse, to courageousness in the declarative chorus. The latter swells into one of the all-time most recognizable rock anthems. If the soaring background vocals are reminiscent of the Beach Boys, it's because Beach Boys Carl Wilson and Bruce Johnston, along with friend Toni Tennille (later famous as half of The Captain and Tennille) performed them.

Figure 6–Intro, Verse 1, Verse 2, Chorus, and Verse 3

The piano intro features a melody that will recur several times later in the song. The intro also uses a series of chord inversions: C, C/B♭, F/A, and C/G. Note how frequently chords in both first and second inversions are used throughout this song.

The verse is built primarily of I, IV, and V chords (C, F, and G). However, these chords are enlivened by the frequent use of gospel-style "amen" embellishment chords. These chords always follow and return to the stationary chord, and are used as ornaments. The embellishment chords occur for only a beat or so, while the stationary chords occur over four or more beats. Most often, the embellishment chords are on "weak" beats. The root of each "amen" chord is a 4th above the root of the chord it ornaments; in traditional music theory, the IV–I cadence is called the plagal or "amen" cadence.

To illustrate: the C triad on the "and" of beat 4 in measure 5 embellishes the more stationary G chord that comes before and after. In measure 8, the F chord on beat 1 embellishes the more stationary C chord. In measure 11, the C triad embellishes the more stationary G chord. Elton John uses this device throughout this song and often in other songs.

Most of the piano fills are based on broken chord patterns, such as the fill in measure 7 on the C chord. The fill in measures 15–16 will recur at measures 23–24 and 32.

The third verse makes use of blues licks. Those in measures 60 and 62 come straight out of the New Orleans piano tradition exemplified by Professor Longhair and Dr. John.

Fig. 6

All my pic-tures _____ seem to fade _ to black _ and white. _

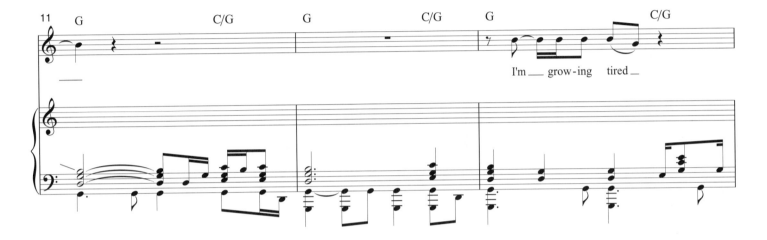

I'm _ grow-ing tired _

and time stands still be-fore _____ me, _

fro - zen here _ on the lad - der of __ my _ life.

Verse 1:08

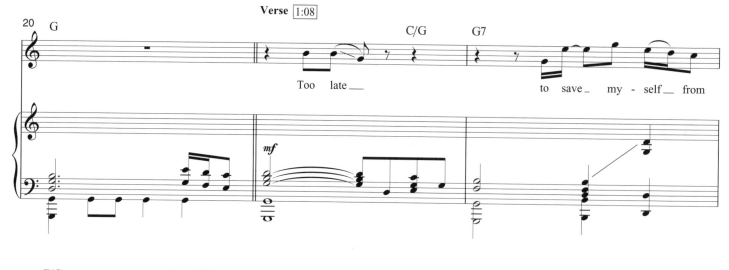

Too late ___ to save ___ my-self ___ from

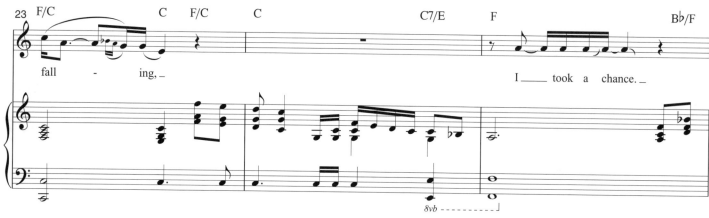

fall - ing, ___ I ___ took a chance. ___

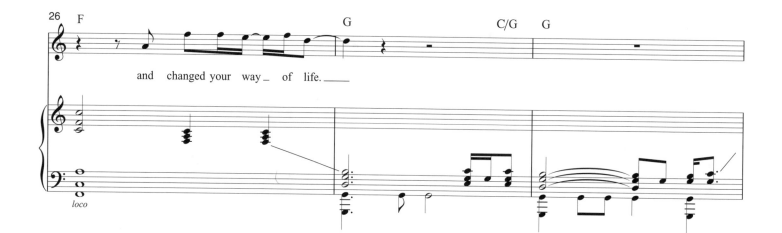

and changed your way ___ of life. ___

But you mis - read my mean-ing when I ___ met ___ you, ___

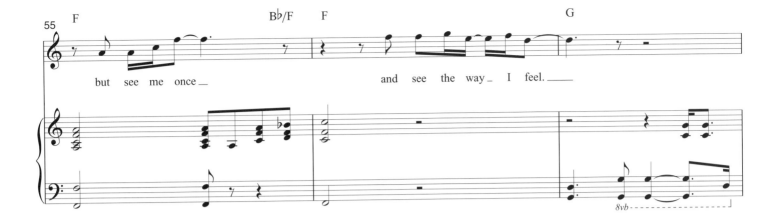

but see me once _____ and see the way _ I feel. _____

Don't dis - card me _____ just be - cause _ you think

I mean you harm. _____ But these cuts _ I _____ have, _____

oh, they need love to help _ them heal. _____

Figure 7–Interlude and Chorus

The piano rhythm becomes more insistent in the chorus, including frequent use of dotted-eighth rhythms and the sixteenth-note triplets at measure 7. The final five measures are a variation of the instrumental intro, with the addition of a dramatic ♭VI–♭VII–I cadence in the last two measures.

Fig. 7

I'd just al - low a frag - ment of ___ your life ___ to wan - der free. ___

yeah, ___ but los - ing eve - ry - thing is like the

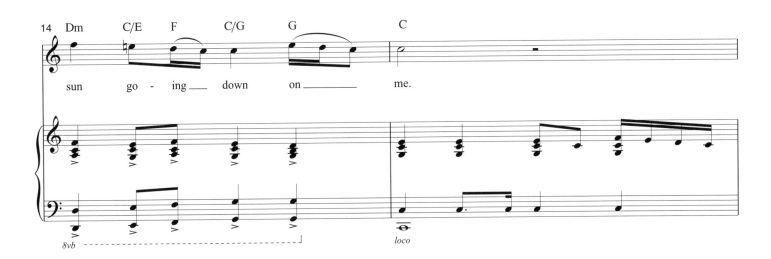

sun go - ing ___ down on ___ me.

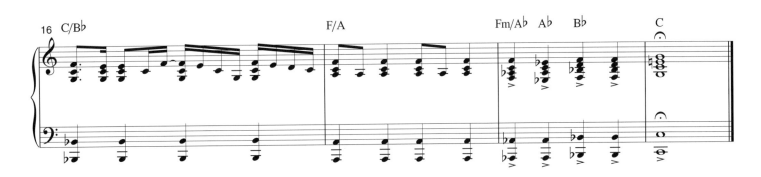

I'D DO ANYTHING FOR LOVE (BUT I WON'T DO THAT)

From the Meat Loaf album
Bat Out of Hell II: Back Into Hell (1993)
Words and Music by Jim Steinman

Meat Loaf was born Marvin Lee Aday in Dallas, Texas. At age 13, because of his enormous size and ungainly manner, his football coach christened him "Meat Loaf." He appeared in *Hair* on Broadway, in the cult film *The Rocky Horror Picture Show*, and in the *National Lampoon Road Show*, where he met songwriter Jim Steinman. Their album collaboration *Bat Out of Hell* hit the top of the charts in 1978. Meat Loaf's subsequent career sputtered until he again teamed up with Steinman for the 1993 stylistic clone *Bat Out of Hell II*. The grandiose, over-the-top arrangements again struck a nerve with the public, and "I'd Do Anything for Love (But I Won't Do That)" rose to #1.

Figure 8–Instrumental Vamp, Verse 1, Verse 2, Pre-Chorus, and Chorus

The instrumental vamp foreshadows the vocal melody of the chorus. It features driving eighth notes in the left hand and I, IV, and V harmonies in the right. The verse switches to the relative minor (B minor) and features interesting open voicings in the piano.

The *voicing* of a chord is essentially the chord shape. A voicing includes how the notes of the chord are arranged vertically, how they are spaced, whether any notes in the chord are doubled, and whether the chord is in root position or an inversion. The voicings in this song, especially on the Gsus2 and Em11 chords (meas. 15, 17, 23, 25, etc.), are very rich and colorful. Chord voicings can be an expressive device in their own right.

The pre-chorus briefly changes to a half-time feel. The harmonies get a little more intense, especially with the use of a diminished 7th chord at measure 39. At measures 43–44 the tempo gradually slows down going into the chorus. The chorus harmony is basically I–IV–V, but is bolstered by the use of a pedal tone D and a nice voicing on the A/D and Gadd9/D chords at measures 51–52.

Note: The timings, sections, and measure numbers here refer to the album version of nearly twelve minutes—not the shortened single.

Gmaj7　A

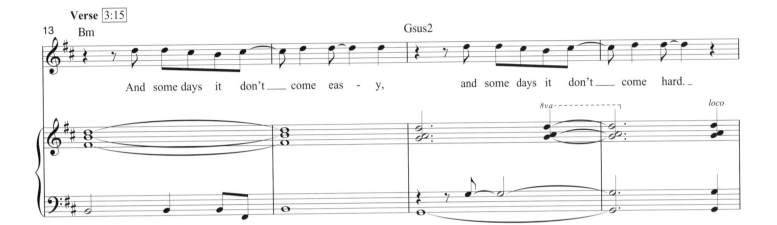

Verse 3:15

And some days it don't ___ come eas - y, and some days it don't ___ come hard. _

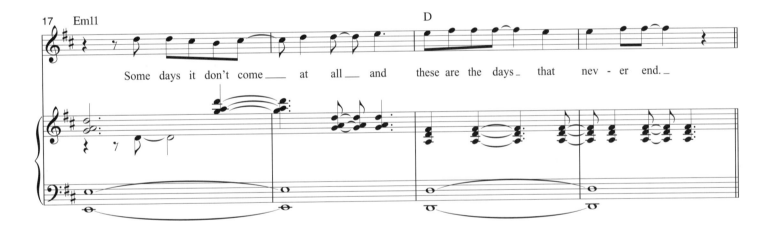

Some days it don't come ___ at all __ and these are the days _ that nev - er end. _

Verse 3:28

And some nights you're breath - ing fire, _ and some nights you're carved _ in ice. _

as long as your dreams ____ are com - ing true, you bet - ter be - lieve ____

Chorus 408
Slower ♩ = 100

____ it that I would do an - y - thing ___ for love, and I'll be there till the

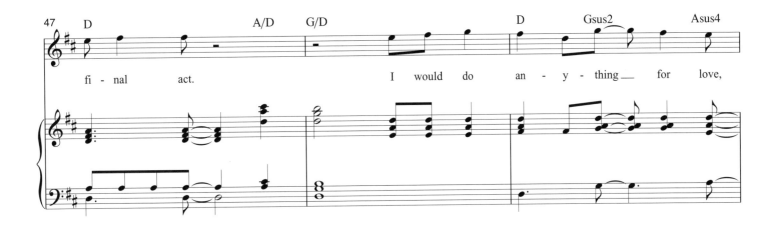

fi - nal act.   I would do an - y - thing ___ for love,

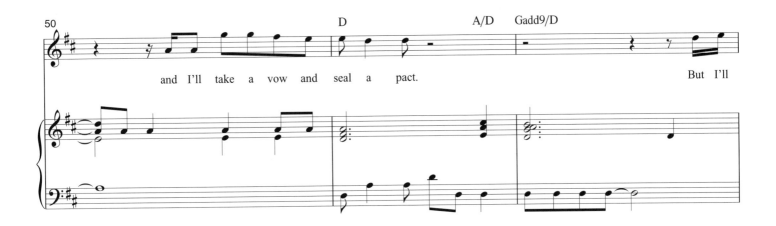

and I'll take a vow and seal a pact.   But I'll

KILLER QUEEN
From the Queen album *Sheer Heart Attack* (1974)
Words and Music by Freddie Mercury

Formed in London in 1972, Queen successfully combined elements of 1970s British glam-rock with 1960s heavy rock (à la Led Zeppelin). Onstage, vocalist/keyboardist Freddie Mercury (born Farok Bulsara in Zanzibar, Tanzania) embodied an outrageous theatricality unmatched in rock. Tragically, he died of complications related to AIDS in 1991. "Killer Queen" is an infectious slice of high camp that reached #2 in 1974.

Figure 9–Intro, Verse, and Chorus

The song begins with a pattern of triads and 7th chords in short, punctuated accents on each beat, played in the alto register by the right hand. The key alternates freely between C minor and E♭ major. At measure 11, the pattern changes to a rolling figure that has a jaunty English music-hall feel. Note the use of secondary dominant chords such as G7 and D7 for added color. The biggest harmonic surprise is the figure in measure 22 consisting of F, B♭/F, and E♭/F.

16	Full Band
17	Slow Demo meas. 11-13, 19-25

Fig. 9

just like __ Ma - rie An - toi - nette. __ A built in __ a - re - me - dy __ for

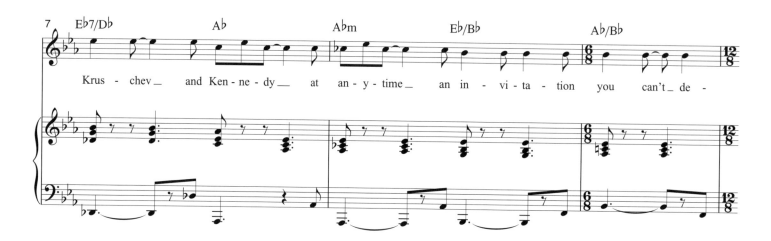

Krus - chev __ and Ken - ne - dy __ at an - y - time __ an in - vi - ta - tion you can't __ de -

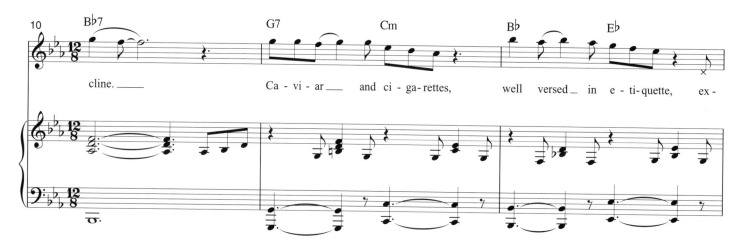

cline. __ Ca - vi - ar __ and ci - ga - rettes, well versed __ in e - ti - quette, ex -

Chorus 0:27

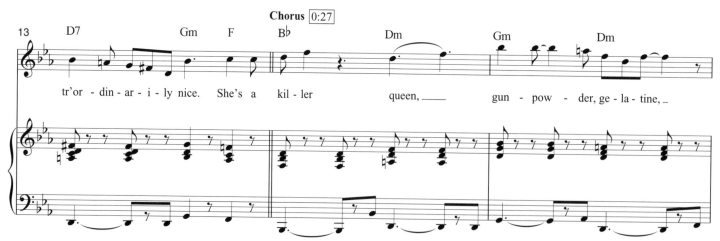

tr'or - din - ar - i - ly nice. She's a kil - ler queen, __ gun - pow - der, ge - la - tine, __

36

dy - na - mite__ with a la - ser beam.__ N' gua - ran - teed__ to blow__ your mind.__

___ Ooh,__ re - com - mend - ed at the price,__ in -

sa - tia - ble an ap - pe - tite.__ Wan - na try?__

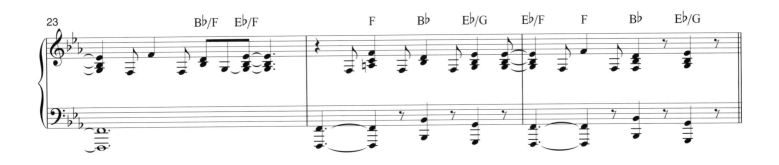

LADY MADONNA
Released as a Beatles single in 1968
Words and Music by John Lennon and Paul McCartney

"Lady Madonna" is a fun rocker with Paul McCartney singing in an overt Elvis Presley imitation and playing raucous boogie-woogie piano in the style of Fats Domino. The lyrics are a bit cryptic. Does Lady Madonna "make ends meet" by prostituting herself? It's unclear. In any case, she is obviously a single mother who has day-to-day concerns with money and paying the rent. Thus, she invites our sympathy.

Ringo achieved a great sound by using brushes on the drums, and the song also features some fine saxophone work.

Figure 10–Intro, Verse 1, Chorus, Verse 2, and Interlude

The boogie-woogie piano part is built on almost constant walking octaves in the left hand, with occasional passing notes (such as C–C♯–D in meas. 1). The right hand alternates between a minor 3rd and a major 3rd on each A chord, giving the song a bluesy feel.

The F–G–A progression at the end of each four-measure phrase in the verse also sounds bluesy, especially in measure 4, when the alternation between major and minor 3rds appears as a grace note.

The chorus unexpectedly jumps into the key of C before returning to the original key (A) for the second verse.

Fig. 10

| 18 | Full Band |
| 19 | Slow Demo
meas. 1-4, 13-20 |

*Chord symbols reflect basic harmony.

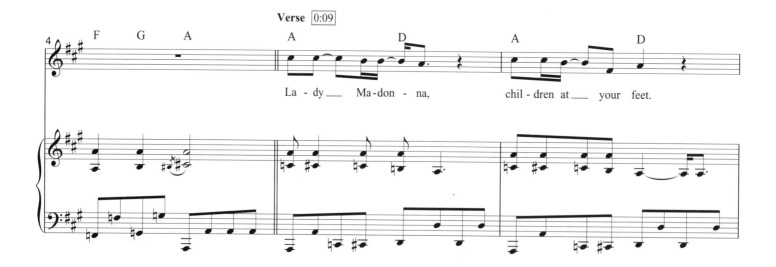

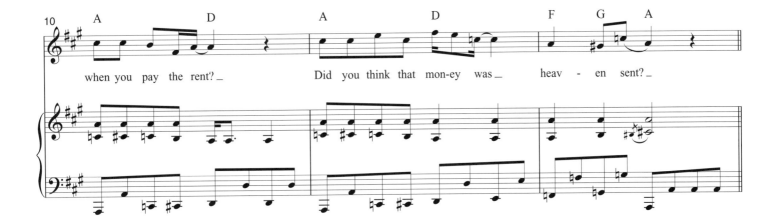

Figure 11–Last Verse and Coda

The coda, beginning at measure 5, adds some new harmonic material that further adds to the bluesy feel. The A major chord contains the minor 3rd as a grace note. The Cm6 chord contains two "blue notes" (notes particular to the A blues scale)—C♮ and E♭.

20 Full Band

21 Slow Demo
meas. 5-8

Fig. 11

LIGHT MY FIRE
From the album *The Doors* (1967)
Words and Music by The Doors

The Doors took their name from a memoir about a mescaline trip by Aldous Huxley entitled "The Doors of Perception" (the title of which cribbed a line from the poetry of William Blake). Formed in Los Angeles in 1965, the Doors had a number of contrasting influences. Keyboardist Ray Manzarek was into blues, drummer John Densmore was studying jazz, guitarist Robbie Krieger had played with a jug band, and vocalist Jim Morrison was inspired by English and Celtic poetry.

"Light My Fire" was primarily the work of Robbie Krieger and was in fact the first song he ever wrote. Manzarek came up with the neoclassical organ introduction, and Densmore added the modified Latin beat. Morrison's sole contribution to the song was the typically dark line, "our love become a funeral pyre." The seven-minute album version was heavily edited for the #1 single.

Figure 12– Intro, Verse, and Chorus

The Doors didn't have a bass player. While a session bassist was often hired for studio recordings, in concert Ray Manzarek played the bass line with his left hand on a Rhodes bass keyboard that sat atop his Vox Continental organ. The left-hand bass line here is built entirely of broken triads and is very suitable for keyboard bass.

"Light My Fire" opens with its signature organ introduction—a quasi-classical swirl of seemingly unrelated major chords in broken chord figures and scale fragments. The verse is harmonically ambiguous. It begins with the odd alternation between A♭m7 and Fm7 chords. The right hand of the organ plays chords in a slightly syncopated rhythm that goes well with the modified Latin drum beat.

At the chorus, the harmony becomes a more conventional IV–V–I in D♭ major using broken chords. There is another harmonic detour, however, as the chorus ends on an E♭ major chord.

Fig. 12

Come on ba - by, light my fire. _____ Try to set the night on

fi - re. _____

Figure 13–Organ Solo

The lengthy organ solo (which was excised from the shortened single version) is built entirely on the alternation of two chords—A♭m7 and B♭m7. It is in the A♭ Dorian mode (A♭–B♭–C♭–D♭–E♭–F–G♭–A♭).

The solo twists and writhes. Measure 5 features the use of a sliding grace note to an insistently repeated B♭. The turn at measure 6–7 gives the solo both a classical touch and a Far Eastern flavor. (A *turn* is a familiar keyboard ornament found in the works of J.S. Bach and other baroque composers.) The solo slowly builds in intensity, partly by gradually moving higher and higher in the keyboard register. Measures 13–14 illustrate how a solo lick can be built out of just two alternating notes when played in an interesting rhythm. Measures 21–24 illustrate a similar point using just three alternating notes.

Measure 29 introduces parallel 3rds in stepwise motion, gradually moving upward. At measure 45, Manzarek plays four-note seventh chords in the right hand, and at measure 51 he returns to parallel 3rds. In measure 56 the entire band plays cascading quarter-note triplets. Organ and guitar lines move up and down in contrary motion in a great climax to a great solo.

Fig. 13

24 Full Band

25 Slow Demo
meas. 1-70

Organ Solo 1:06

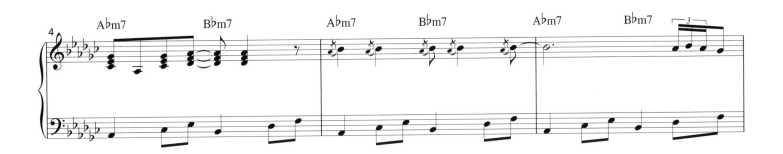

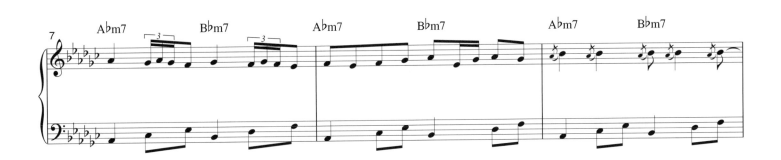

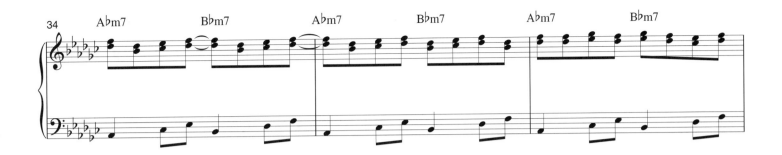

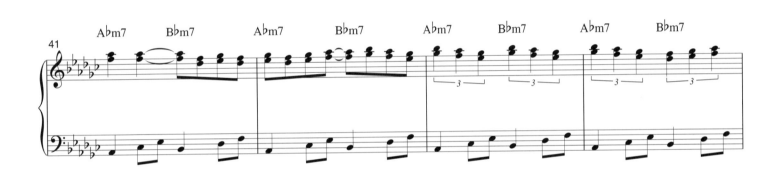

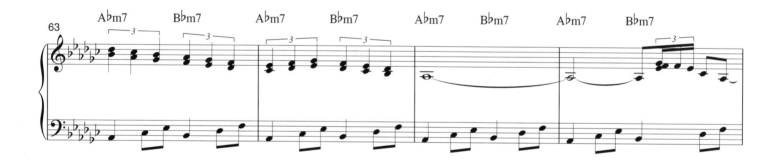

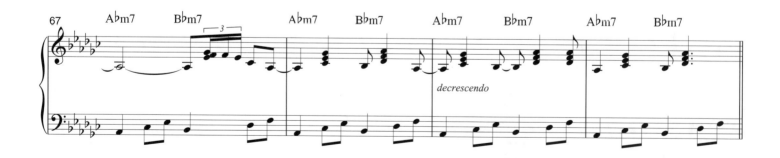

PIANO MAN

From the Billy Joel album *Piano Man* (1973)
Words and Music by Billy Joel

After releasing his first solo album, Billy Joel "hid out and killed time" in Los Angeles, where he played cocktail piano incognito for six months (under the name Bill Martin) at a watering hole called The Executive Cocktail Lounge. This experience formed the basis for his 1973 hit single "Piano Man." Ironically, Joel's sardonic view from the piano bench of the bar's losers, wannabes, and has-beens has become the anthem of piano bars everywhere.

Figure 14–Intro

The intro begins with a short cocktail piano flourish in free time. Measure 3 introduces the main feel—a bright waltz in insistent "oom-pah-pah" rhythm. (The harmonica lead is not notated here.) The chords are fairly primary, mainly I, IV, and V, and the bass line descends diatonically, creating several slash chords. The D7 chord provides a little extra color, and the piano passage in measures 17–20 is pretty slick.

26 Full Band

27 Slow Demo
meas. 17-20

Figure 15–Verse

The verse continues the straight waltz pattern. Accordion is introduced at measure 23. The second part of the verse is essentially the first part with the vocal melody raised one octave.

Fig. 15

28 Full Band

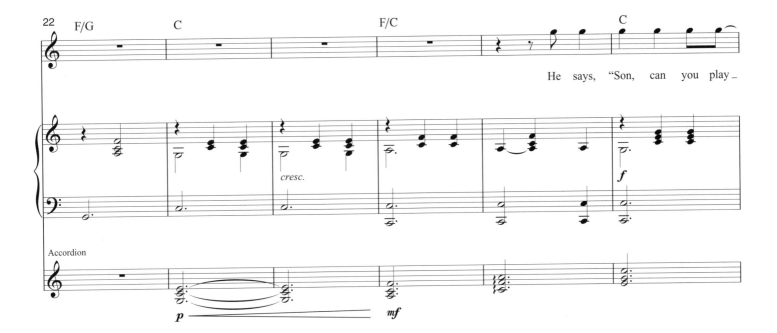

Figure 16–Pre-Chorus

The pre-chorus section switches to A minor, a descending bass line, and "la la's" in the vocal. The chorus (not shown) is musically identical to the verse, which is quite unusual for a pop song.

Figure 17–Piano Interlude

The piano improvises briefly in the interlude over a pattern of Am–Am/G–D–F. The right hand runs, such as the one in measure 9, make use of the A blues scale (A–C–D–E♭–E–G–A).

Fig. 17

Interlude 3:25

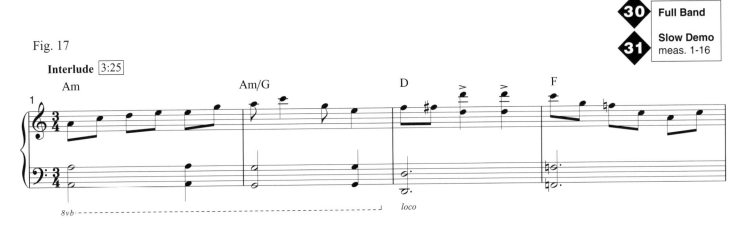

POINT OF KNOW RETURN

From the Kansas album *Point of Know Return* (1977)

Words and Music by Steve Walsh, Phil Ehart and Robert Steinhardt

The six-man band Kansas was formed in 1972 in Topeka, Kansas. For most of their career they were a windswept mid-American answer to British progressive rock groups such as Yes and Genesis.

Figure 18–Intro

The intro features piano and organ in a syncopated chord pattern of F–Cm–E♭–B♭sus4–F over a tonic F pedal. This pattern is repeated four times.

32	**Full Band**
33	**Slow Demo** Piano meas. 5-8

Fig. 18

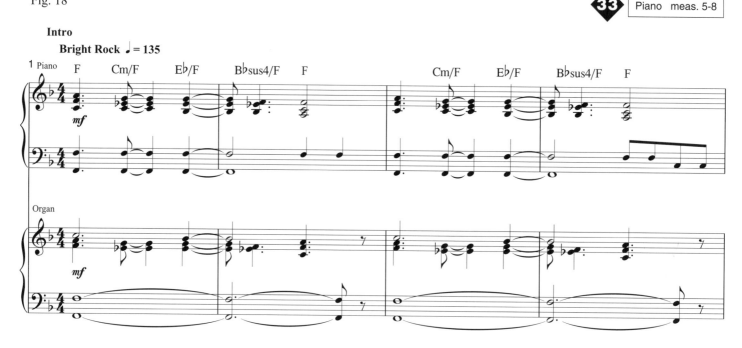

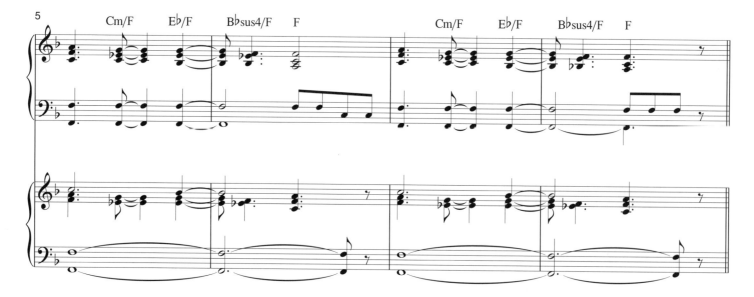

Figure 19–Verse 2, Chorus, Interlude, and Bridge

The second verse features piano and organ. The organ plays triads in the soprano register of the keyboard. These chords are mainly I, IV, and V, but syncopated rhythms and an occasional odd measure of 3/4 enliven the pattern. The piano plays the same chords, with the extra flourish of broken chords used as fills.

At the chorus (meas. 10), the piano plays accented punches on the words "how long," while the organ fills in with quick broken chords on B♭, C, and F. The violin doubles the organ fills. These chords all lie comfortably within the span of the right hand and can be played with fingers 1, 3, and 5. At measure 14, both the piano and the organ play triads in the right hand, with bass notes or octaves in the left. Measures 16 and 17 are a repeat of the intro figure.

The interlude features the organ in a harmonically colorful passage of chords totally unrelated to the key of F. First there are triads in the right hand over a pedal C# resolving to an E chord. Then the entire passage is repeated a 4th higher. The solo violin has the lead one octave above the organ, and a single-line synth part is added in between the organ and the violin.

The bridge finds us in the key of G with a half-time feel in the drums. The organ holds triads, and the piano plays chords on beats 1 and 3.

34 **Full Band**

35 **Slow Demo**
Piano meas. 5-10
Organ meas. 10-11

Fig. 19

- mons guard__ is an o- cean grave for all_____ the brave. Was it

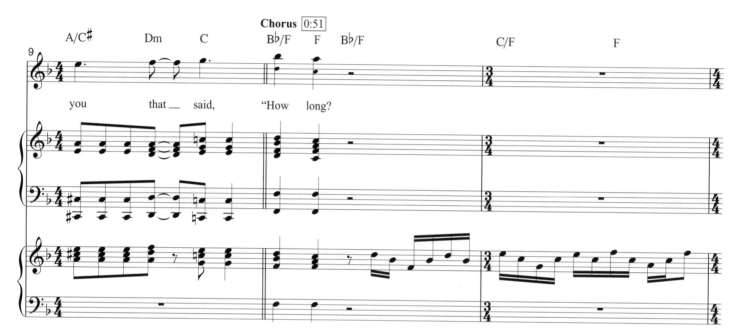

you that__ said, "How long?

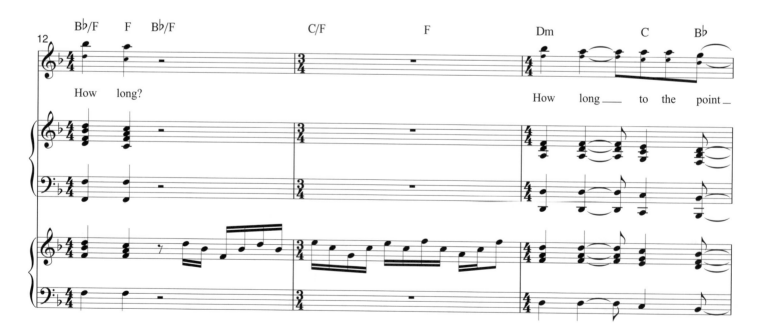

How long? How long____ to the point__

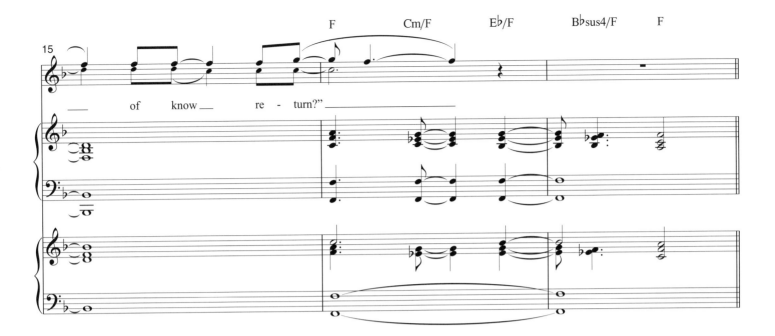

of know ____ re - turn?" _____

Interlude 1:04

Bridge 1:25

Synth. and Violin tacet

Your fa - ther, he said he needs _____ you. _____

Piano

Organ

Your moth - er, she said she loves _____ you. _____

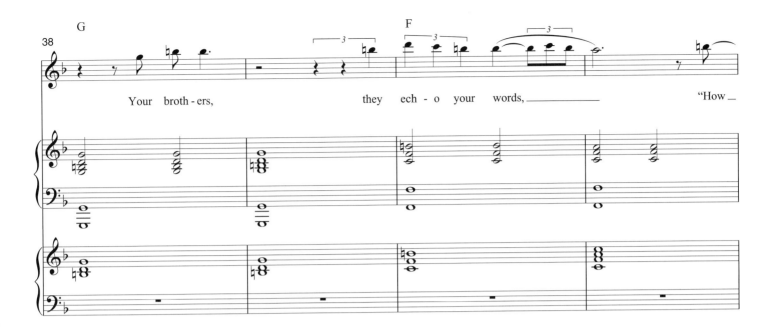

Your broth-ers, they ech-o your words, _____ "How _

_ far _ to the point of know _ re - turn, _____ to the
(Point of know _ re - turn.) _

point of know _ re - turn?" _____ Well, how long?

SEPARATE WAYS
(WORLDS APART)

From the Journey album *Frontiers* (1983)
Words and Music by Steve Perry and Jonathan Cain

Former members of Santana formed Journey in San Francisco in 1973. Keyboardist Jonathan Cain joined the group in 1981, and "Separate Ways" was a hit single shortly thereafter in 1983.

Figure 20–Intro and Verse

The song begins with an Em broken chord figure played by synthesizer in the soprano register. The synth plays solo for four measures before the band enters at measure 5. The synth features a biting metallic sound with the decay set so that a note decays (i.e., fades out) after approximately four beats.

The synth part changes to simple held triads in the alto range at measure 9 over a constantly pounding E pedal in the bass. This pattern continues during the verse.

The next verse pattern, beginning at measure 28, introduces some other harmonies, including the colorful sonority of G/C in measure 29.

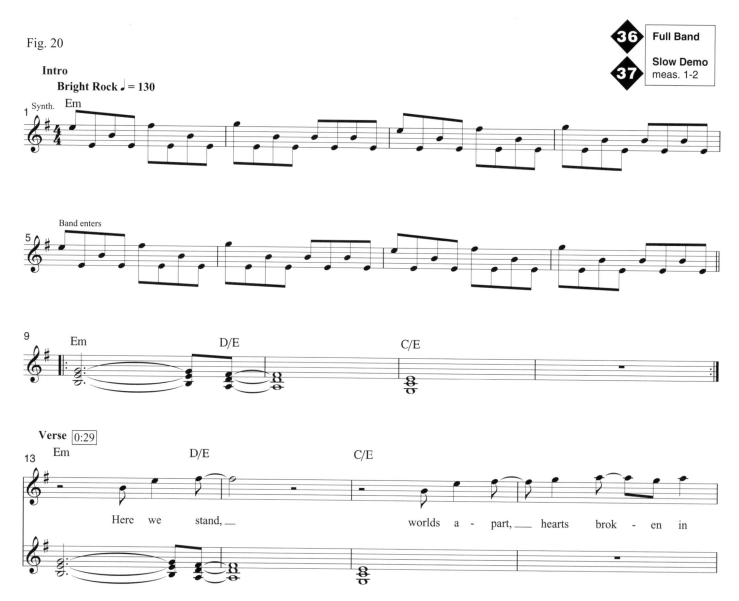

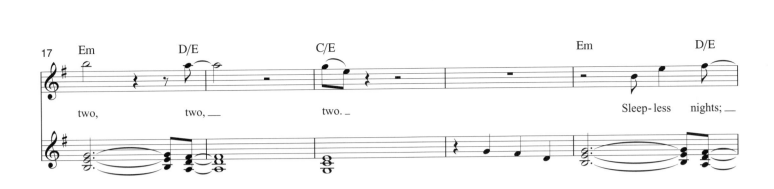

two, two,   two.   Sleep-less nights;

los - ing ground   I'm reach - in' for   you, you,

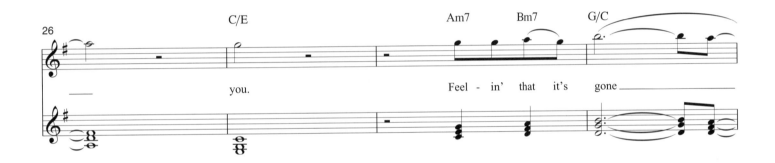

you. Feel - in' that it's gone

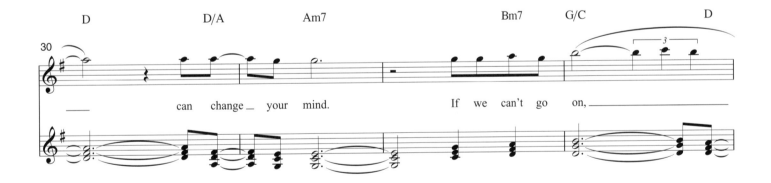

can change   your mind. If we can't go on,

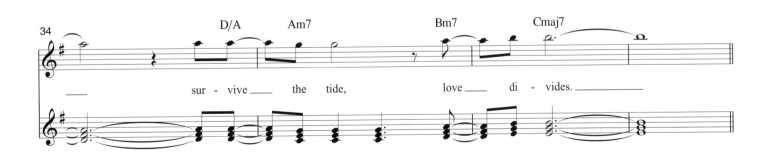

sur - vive   the tide, love   di - vides.

Figure 21–Instrumental Interlude

The instrumental interlude features two synthesizer parts. Synth 1 plays the same Em broken chord pattern from the intro. This pattern is now embellished by the addition of changing intervals of a 5th in the left hand: E5, G5, C5, and A5. At measure 9, the lead synth (using a crystalline patch) plays a very simple melody line in the high soprano register consisting of just four notes: E, B, A, and G.

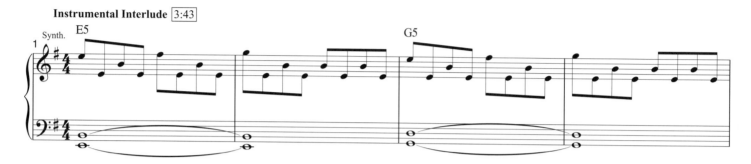

38 Full Band

Fig. 21

Instrumental Interlude 3:43

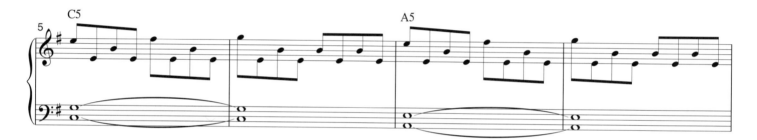

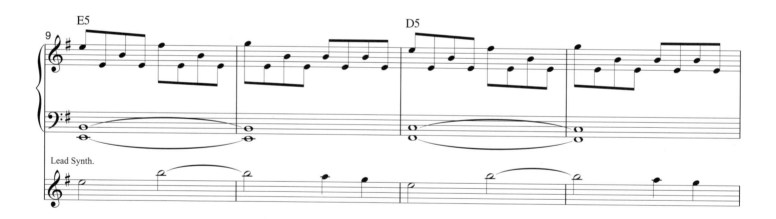

WEREWOLVES OF LONDON
From the Warren Zevon album *Excitable Boy* (1978)
Words and Music by Warren Zevon, Robert Wachtel and LeRoy Marinel

Warren Zevon began his career in the 1960s writing songs for the Turtles and other groups and serving as touring musical director for the Everly Brothers. Linda Ronstadt covered several of his songs in the 1970s. Zevon's L.A.-noir writing style invites comparisons to the twisted narratives of Randy Newman.

Figure 22—Intro, Verse, and Chorus

This song is a good example of using an economy of musical ideas for maximum effect. The introduction features a two-measure, three-chord piano pattern that, repeated over and over, will be the basis of the entire song. The chords are simple: D (V), C (IV), and G (I). None of the chords possess a 3rd, and that gives them an open feel. The left hand plays octave roots, while the right-hand pattern is enlivened by the use of a 6th resolving into each chord. For example, B to A is used over the D chord, A to G over the C chord, etc.

The chorus, with its signature werewolf howl of "ow-ooh," is based on the same chords.

39 Full Band

40 Slow Demo
meas. 1-2

Fig. 22

rain. He was look - in' for the place called Li - Ho Fook's

Chorus 0:37

for to get a big dish of beef chow mein. Ow - ooh,

were - wolves of Lon - don. Ow - ooh.

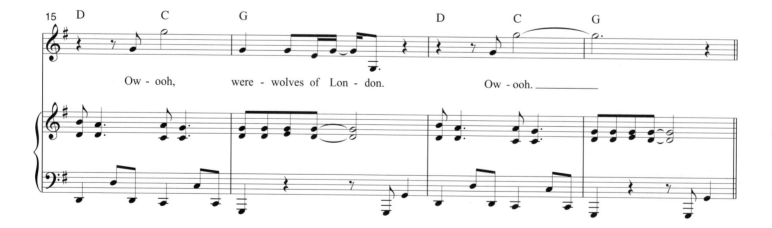

Ow - ooh, were - wolves of Lon - don. Ow - ooh.